Go Away, S

Story by
Sally Cowan

Illustrations by
Anne Spudvilas

"It is very hot today," said Rosa.
"The birds will like this new bird bath."

"Yes," said Dad.
"Birds like to splash in water."

A little bird came flying down from the tree.
It went into the bird bath.

Splash! Splash! Splash!

"Look, Dad!" cried Rosa.

"Socks is outside.

He is hiding in the leaves.

The little bird can't see him!"

The little bird saw Dad
and it went up into the sky.

Socks hid in the leaves again.

"Naughty Socks!" said Rosa. "Please go away from here."

But Socks stayed in the leaves by the bird bath.

"Dad, can the bird bath go here by the house?" said Rosa. "The birds will see Socks coming out of the leaves, and they will fly away."

Rosa helped Dad with the bird bath.

"Look at the birds," said Rosa.
"They are splashing in the water."

"You are clever, Rosa," said Dad.

"The birds are safe from you, Socks!" said Rosa.